FLIGHT

A *terra magica* BOOK

JACQUES F. ORMOND

FLIGHT

WITH A PREFACE BY JEAN COCTEAU

HILL AND WANG · NEW YORK

Published in the United States of America by Hill and Wang, Inc., 1963. Library of Congress catalog card number: 63-18450. © 1962 Hanns Reich Verlag, Munich. All rights reserved, including those of photographic reproduction, reprint in whole or in part, and diffusion by radio and television. Printed in Switzerland.

PREFACE

I once remarked to Gabriel Voisin that even the most modern airplanes struck me as outdated and that I wondered why. He explained to me that this was because the airplane is based on the principle of the wing. This, he felt, was just as if the first automobiles had been built with mechanical paws instead of wheels. In the entire field of aeronautics there was nothing that compared to the brilliant invention of the wheel.

We ought to forget the unfortunate line of development of the airplane and admit that man's flight should have nothing in common with that of birds. Step by step, airplane wings must be made shorter, until they have been altogether eliminated and a completely new start can be made.

It is astonishing that a genius like Leonardo da Vinci should have insisted that a flying machine must be heavier than air—in imitation of the bird; as an artist, imitation should have been farthest from his mind.

In brief, man has not yet found the right idea; he still needs the proper machine—in which many skeptics refuse to believe—to rise from the ground without effort, thus severing the umbilical cord that ties him to Mother Earth. When he succeeds in discovering antigravity and conquering the mysterious gravitational pull of earth, when he can change the phenomenon of falling into genuine flight, only then will

5

man cease to be a big clumsy bird and will assume the same predominant position in the air which he believes himself to be occupying on earth.

This enchanting picture book shows immobilized speed—speed that has become a picture. While poor Icarus is still flying, the photographer catches him and so lends everlasting life to his fugitive passage; just as Japanese artists solve the problem of time by magically unrolling their painted scrolls.

Between each stanza of his ornithological poems, the photographer shows us a feather, delicate as the hair of angels. And again, speed is turned into a statue, which makes it even more exhilarating. We experience the felicitous union of science and poetry. Let me close with an enigmatic sentence by Apollinaire, which I have also quoted in my film "Orphée": "The bird sings with its fingers." For, everything about the bird remains a mystery to us: from its ruthless cruelty to its heavenly song. The ancient Greeks knew what they were doing when they represented the mythical creatures of their legends in the venerable form of birds.

JEAN COCTEAU

INTRODUCTION

Since time immemorial it has been man's dream to soar to the skies. The urge to rise above our natural condition is always alive in us. Our ancestors mingled imagination with reality: they made the bird a symbol of man's soul. Among the cave paintings in Lascaux, which date back nearly forty thousand years, there is a picture of a man who has been killed by a bull; a bird beside the dead man undoubtedly represents the soul of the departed.

In our time, technology has found ways of building birds of steel that carry us aloft. But metallic wings have not been able to assuage man's yearning to rise above his own humdrum existence. Although the bird no longer symbolizes man's soul for us, the sight of his light wings still makes us dream of being able to fly as he flies.

When I first began to photograph birds, such thoughts were far from my mind. I liked birds and enjoyed hearing them sing and watching them fly. More than twenty-five years have passed since that Sunday in October when I gaily set out to look for snipe. I was cheerful because the weather was fine and I was armed not only with a rifle but with a simple pocket-size kodak camera as well. I had made up my mind that I would photograph a snipe in flight—naive beginner that I was.

The next day, when I studied my carefully finished prints—on which, of course, no trace of the snipe could be seen—I began to realize some of the difficulties connected with the job of photographing birds in flight.

After that first disappointment, I began to replace my photographic equipment, since what I had was inadequate for this type of work. I bought a Leica with a telescopic lens, the indispensable Hector 135-mm. Later I had a special ring made which enabled me to use the Telyt 200-mm. without the clumsy focusing device that came with it in those days.

Though photographic equipment has improved greatly since then, the technique remains the same. The biggest problem is distance. For every bird, depending on its size, there is a limit beyond which the film no longer picks up any of those important details without which the picture will be meaningless. It might be the eye, the beak, the legs, the wing feathers, the precision of the silhouette. You must always catch at least one exact detail. It is the only way to bring the picture to life and make it convincing.

How can the problem of distance be overcome? First of all, the camera must have a tele-lens. That is absolutely necessary when you want to take pictures of birds in flight, especially when you take them near the nest.

The best thing, of course, is to use several lenses of different focal length, depending on the type of shot and the kind of bird you are after. I use four different tele-lenses with my Leica: the Hector 135-mm., which gives me a shutter speed of up to 1/200 second and is especially good for close-ups; then, the handy Telyt 200-mm., with which I have taken most of my pictures; also, the new Telyt of 280-mm. focal length, which serves me well, though it is somewhat bigger and heavier; and, finally, I sometimes use the Telyt 400-mm., which helps me get good shots of hard-to-get-close-to-subjects.

Next, you have to decide how you will get near your quarry. One way is to build a blind. This works especially well during the nesting season, when you can pick out just the right spot. But you must stay motionless and well under cover in your blind. Some birds soon get used to the presence of the photographer and his blind, whether it is made of twigs, reeds, or sailcloth; at least, they act as if they had no idea you are there, and often come quite close to your lens. You work under favorable conditions then. You can set your distance in advance. There is time to view the bird carefully, as it approaches, and you can choose the best moment to release the shutter. But a blind is not always easy to build or comfortable to use; you need a lot of time and patience for it. It is often more practical to stalk a bird to photograph it in flight. In that case, you depend on reducing your distance by stealth and clever methods of approach.

It is hard to say at just what distance it no longer pays to release the shutter. For a bird the size of a gray heron, I would set the limit at about sixty feet, for a duck at forty-five feet; for a stilt at less than thirty feet. Photographing a stilt in flight, at a distance of twenty-five feet is not an easy task. The trick is to release the shutter without viewing. In general, it is easier to aim with a camera than with a gun. You can use any kind of view finder that allows you to hold the camera at eye level and to keep both eyes open—as you would with a hunting rifle.

The focus depends on the distance and lens opening, in other words, on the light which allows you, at a given shutter speed, to enlarge or reduce the depth of field by opening up or stopping down your lens. The depth of field also depends on the focal length of your tele-lens. For instance, at a distance of forty-five feet and with f 6.3, the Hector 135-mm. will give you a depth of several yards, the Telyt 280-mm. only sixty inches, and the Telyt 400-mm. a mere twenty inches.

Exposure times can vary from 1/250 second to 1/1000 second, depending on which tele-lens you are using and how fast the bird moves.

Unfortunately, these exposure times don't permit stopping-down very much; not even if the light is very good. For this reason it is important to use film with extrafine grain which makes maximum enlargement possible. It is regrettable that these films are still not really sensitive enough, though they have been greatly improved in recent years.

In order to take a good picture, it is not enough just to overcome the technical problems of getting close to your subject and setting the camera correctly. You also need luck—plenty of luck. First of all, the subject must be well illuminated: a little sunlight in the right place can bring out the roundness of the body, make the feathers translucent, emphasize an outline. Then, too, you must get the bird in a photogenic pose; for instance, you can't have the head covered by a wing, or the wing on a line with the body. When wing and body merge into a single mass, the bird looks like a projectile. It is impossible to catch the ideal position with exactitude, because the human eye cannot always recognize it in every detail. To release the shutter at the right moment is a matter of luck. You must always take many pictures to get a few good ones.

The background is important, too. It might consist of reeds, a tree, a river bank, a cloud, or a reflection on water. The bird must stand out well against this background. It almost always does when you use water or sky.

Before you begin, you have to work out a plan of attack to help your luck along. Here is where your hunter's instinct should come into play. You have to size up your bird at one glance, as a toreador sizes up his bull. You must sense how close you can come and anticipate the bird's reaction. Study its beak: it might give you a hint in which direction the bird is likely to take off. You must consider wind and vegetation, choose your background, and set your camera.

The picture hunter should say to himself: "I want a photograph of that mallard in flight. Right now it is taking a mud bath beside that pond. If I approach very cautiously on my elbows and knees, I'll get to within thirty or thirty-five feet of the bird before it notices me. I'll set my Telyt 200-mm. for forty-five feet, f 9, 1/500 second. My depth of field begins at forty feet and goes to forty-eight feet. How can I get another eighteen paces closer to the bird? I'll move a few feet to the left to get my camera in line with that clump of reeds that should make an ideal foreground. When the mallard takes to the air, I expect it will be in full sunlight, the sun being on my right. This will give luster to its eyes and emphasize the roundness of its gray belly."

If you are tempted to photograph birds in flight, go to it. It is a sport that can become a passion and provide a vast field of activity. Every bird has an infinite variety of interesting poses; and, besides, there are still plenty of breeds that have never been photographed in flight.

All you need is a little perseverance and... good hunting!

JACQUES F. ORMOND

Translated by Maria Pelikan

Picture captions in fold-out at the back of the book.

...erent sizes in such a way that he began with the smallest feather and kept adding longe...

...and longer ones, so it seemed as if they had grown thus staggered in size. He tied thes...

...eathers together with twine and sealed their underside with beeswax. When he ha...

...secured them in this way, he gave them an almost imperceptible curvature, until the...

...completely resembled a bird's wings.

...Dedalus put the finishing touches to his work, attached the wings to his body, the...

...ound his balance between them and rose into the air like a bird. After he returned t...

...earth, he instructed his young son Icarus, for whom he had fashioned a smaller pair o...

...wings.

...'Always keep to the middle road, my dear son,'' he said, ''so that, should you fly too low...

...your pinions will not graze the ocean waves. Weighed down by moisture, they woul...

...drag you down to the depths of the sea. Nor must you rise to high into the upper regions...

...where your plumage might come too near the rays of the sun and catch fire. Always fl...

...between water and sun, in the wake of my own path through the air.'' Thus speaking...

...Dedalus fastened the wings to his son's shoulders, but while he did so his old hand...

...trembled and a tear fell on his hand. Then he embraced the boy and gave him a kis...

...which proved to be his last.

...Now both rose up on their wings. The father flew ahead, anxious as a bird who takes it...

...brood from the safety of the nest into the hazards of the air for the very first time. All wer...

...well for a while. They passed the isle of Samos on the left, and soon afterward th...

...slands of Delos and Paros. Other coastlines slipped by beneath them. But then the bo...

...Icarus, made confident by the success of his flight, ignored his father's warning and...

...n a spirit of exuberance, rose up into higher regions. But he soon paid for his foo...

...hardiness. The powerful rays of the sun softened the beeswax that held his pinions to...

...gether, and before Icarus became aware of it, the wings dissolved and fell away from bot...

...his shoulders. The wretched youth still waved and swung his bare arms; but he no longe...

...could catch the air in them, and he plummeted into the sea with terrible suddenness...

How I yearn to throw myself into endless space and float above
the awe-ful abyss. JOHANN WOLFGANG VON GOETHE

Let each man ask himself whether he has not felt within his soul
the wish to fly by his own power—and how far removed he is from
daring such an attempt, even in a closed room. LINA LOOS

8

9

14

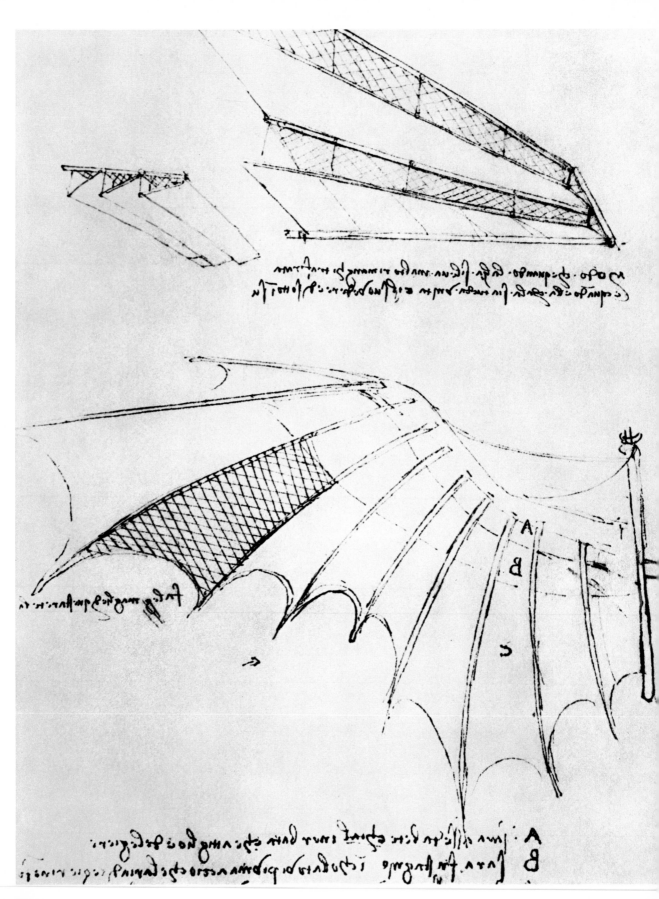

ou see how the eagle's wings, beating against the air, allow him to float in the highest, hinnest region, near the element of fire. And you also see how swiftly the air that moves bove the sea, when caught in the bulging sails, can drive the heavily laden ship forward; om these convincing and definite proofs you realize that man—by pitting his strength gainst the air's resistance and conquering it—could subjugate the air and rise up into on large wings of his own making. A thing exerts as much force against the air as the ir exerts against it.

LEONARDO DA VINCI

There goes a bird,
pushing the clouds aside like useless veils,
he knows no fear of light,
enclosed in flight,
he knows no shadow.

(Un oiseau s'envole
Il rejette les nues comme un voile inutile,
Il n'a jamais craint de la lumière,
Enfermé dans son vol,
Il n'a jamais eu d'ombre.)

PAUL ELUARD

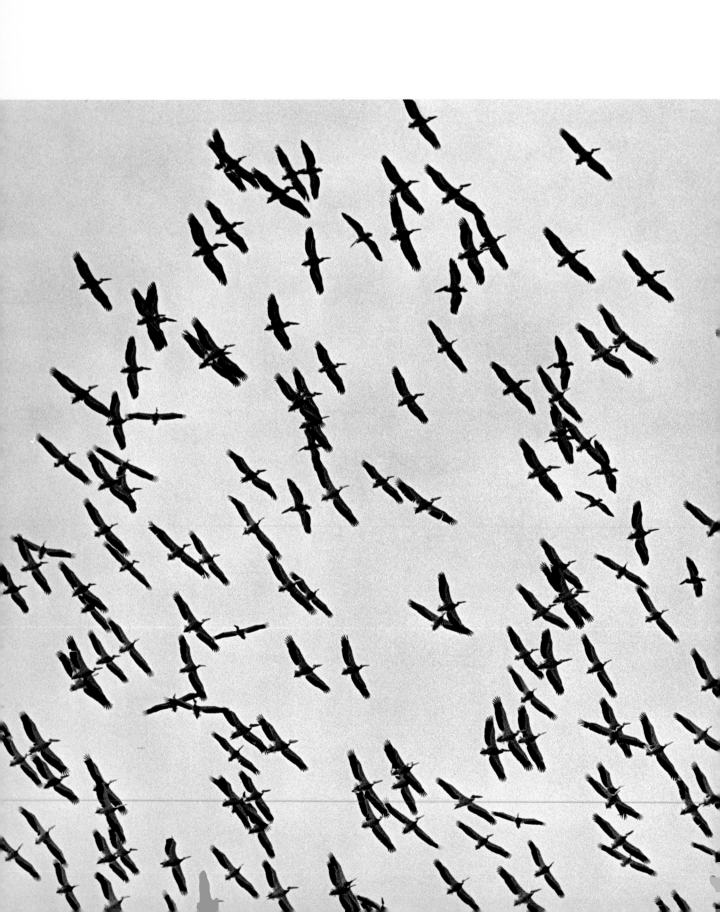

43

44

53

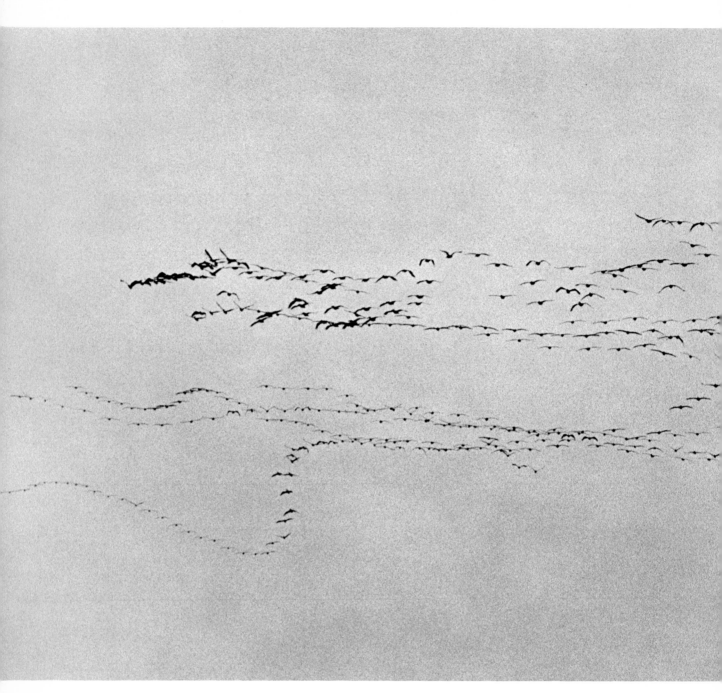

63

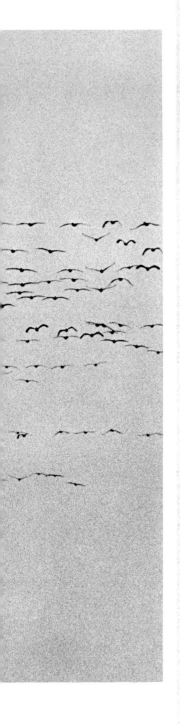

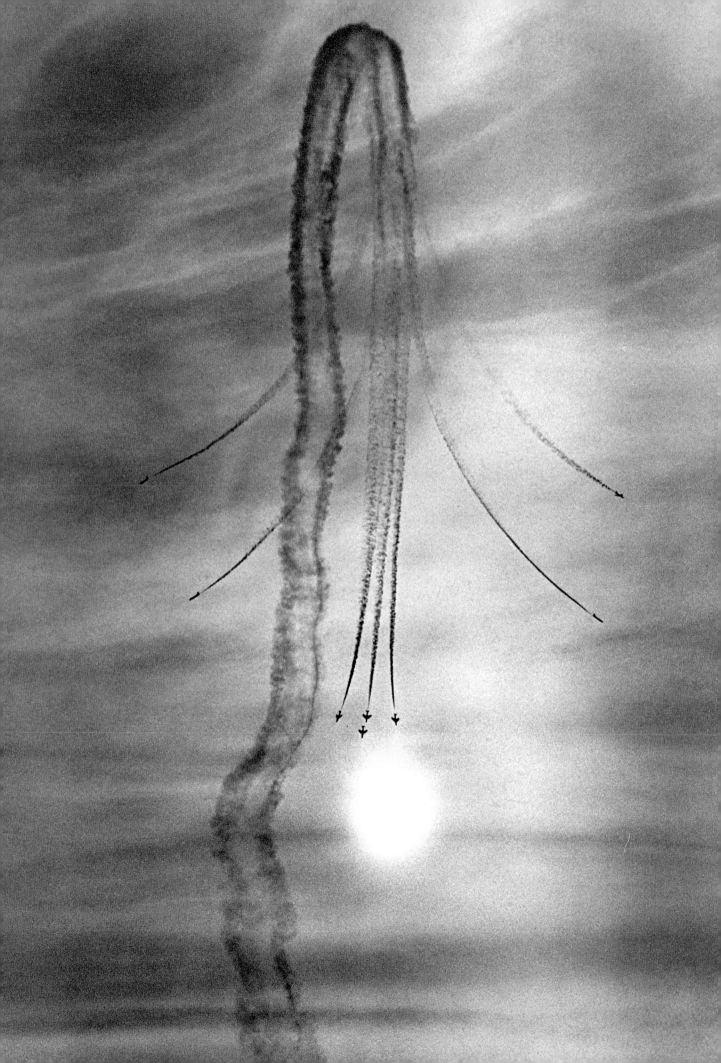

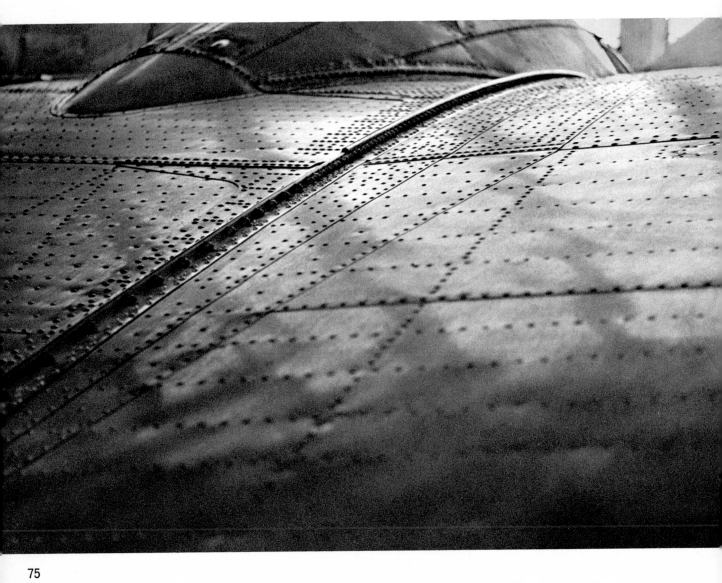

Away from these troubles, from all the pain
That holds our lives in its gray dominion,
Happy is he, who, on powerful pinion,
Can soar toward a fairer, more luminous plain!

His thoughts rising up like larks, he will
Sail in the morning high over the land—
His soul being free, he will understand
The language of flowers and of things that are still!

(Derrière les ennuis et les vastes chagrins
Qui chargent de leur poids l'existence brumeuse,
Heureux celui qui peut d'une aile vigoureuse
S'élancer vers les champs lumineux et sereins!

Celui dont les pensées, comme des alouettes,
Vers les cieux le matin prennent un libre essor,
— Qui plane sur la vie et comprend sans effort
Le langage des fleurs et des choses muettes!)

BAUDELAIRE

Do not boast about the tempo of technology. The final, essential questions are n
altered by technology. They remain. Even in the most modern airplane you travel forev
with yourself—your mood, your misery, your world-weariness. You may be able
measure you blood-pressure more accurately than Albertus Magnus did. In phot
graphs, you may depict landscapes more precisely than Aristotle could. The ultima
questions still stand before your soul today, as they always have. Take heed that yo
flight does not carry you beyond that which is essential, but closer to it.

CARL SONNENSCHEI

88

89

PHOTOGRAPHERS	PICTURES
Hans B. Burgunder	57, 71
Stévan Célébonovic	Endpapers, 4, 28, 41, 70, 76, 82
Arthur Christiansen	62
Deutsches Museum, München	2, 5, 15, 17, 23
Flammarion	19
Gerhard Hanig	85
Foto Heimhuber	7
Theodor Heimgartner	51, 59, 61, 65, 90
Hist. Bildarchiv L. Handke	9, 10
Thomas Höpker – Pontis	31
Laenderpress	16
Mickelsson – I.N.S.	74
Peter Moeschlin	22
Musée de l'Air	21
Jacques F. Ormond	Cover photographs, 1, 3, 11, 12, 20, 24, 25, 26, 27, 29, 30, 32, 33, 34, 35, 36, 37, 39, 40, 42, 43, 45, 46, 47, 48, 49, 50, 52, 53, 54, 55, 56, 58, 60, 63, 64, 68, 69, 72, 73, 75, 77, 78, 79, 80, 81, 83, 84, 87, 89, 91, 92
Paris-Match Archiv	88
Hanns Reich	6
Ringier-Bilderdienst	44
Hans W. Silvester	13, 14
Rudi Stümpel – Bavaria	67
USIS	86
Vogel – Anthony	38
Ludwig Windstoßer – Bavaria	8
Walter Wissenbach	18, 66

Pictures 19 and 21 from: Chambe, Histoire de l'Aviation, Librairie E. Flammarion.

CAPTIONS

Please fold out ▶

24. Pink-headed dove *(Streptopelia decaocto roseogrisa)*. This very light-colored dove lives in large flocks in tropical Africa. It is closely related to the Turkish dove which has recently immigrated to Europe from the southeast; wing span about 16 in.; weight about 5 oz. Photographed near Fort Lamy on the Schari.

25. A little egret rises from the ground (see cover); in the background, a marabou *(Leptopilus crumeniferus)*.

26. Little egret (see cover).

27. Snakebird or darter *(Anhinga rufa)*. Related to the cormorants; lives in tropical Africa; plumage black with metallic green sheen; neck brown; length 34 in.; wing span over 40 in.; can be found near all kinds of water; swims with its body submerged so that only the head and neck show; pointed, dagger-sharp bill. Photographed near Fort Richard-Toll, Senegal.

28. Tail feathers, six times enlarged.

29. Mallard or wild duck *(Anas platyrhynchos)*. This ancestor of the domesticated duck is somewhat smaller in size; weight 22 to 28 oz.; the most common of European wild ducks; the drake has splendid coloring during breeding season; this semimigratory bird travels south but seldom crosses the Sahara. Photographed in Camargue.

30. Crowned crane *(Balearica pavonina)*. One of the most decorative birds of tropical Africa. Plumage bluish-black and white; wings brown and light yellow; feather crown golden yellow. Wing span 76 in.; length 40 in.; weight 178 oz. Photograph from Wasa, northern Cameroon.

31. Glider plane.

32. One of the large species of African vultures. With their length of more than 40 in. and a wing span of up to 112 in., they are among the largest birds in the world. They live exclusively on carrion. Photograph from Wasa, northern Cameroon.

33. Yellow-billed egret *(Mesophoyx intermedius)*. Larger than the little egret and smaller than the great white heron; snow-white, as are all egrets; bill yellow; no neck feathers; legs black except for upper thighs, which are yellow; breeds in tropical Africa. Photographed at the Logone, Chad.

34. Darter (see 27).

35-36. Little egret (see cover).

37. Rosy gray pelican *(Pelecanus onocrotalus)*. Very large clumsy bird; weight 350 to 430 oz.; length up to 72 in.; span 80 to 100 in.; bill 16 in. with characteristic yellow pouch; can be found in Europe in the Danube delta and the southwestern Balkans; otherwise in Africa and southern Asia; breeds in large colonies. Photographed at Boon-Doom, Senegal.

38. The glider soars with the ease and grace of a bird. This is the fulfillment of the dream of flying.

39. Pheasant *(Phasianus colchicus)*. Weight about 35 oz.; the cock is splendidly multicolored; hens and chicks have gray-brown protective coloring with dark spots. Originally indigenous to western Asia, the pheasant was brought to Europe in the early Middle Ages. Shown here are young birds; they leave the nest and are able to fly at the age of twelve days. Photographed at Brieux, Les Dombes (Ain, France).

40. Vulture (see 32).

41. The feathers of an exotic bird, ten times enlarged.

42. Night heron (see 1). This young bird still shows the characteristic streaked plumage.

43. White stork *(Ciconia ciconia)*. Length 40 in.; span 90 in.; weight 110 to 155 oz. This well-loved bird is all white except for black wing-tips; bill and legs red; breeds in Europe; goes south in winter, as far as East and South Africa. Photographed in northern Kenya, near Isiolo.

44. The glider plane floats through the air like a bird.

45. Darter (see 27).

46. Saddle bird or jabiru *(Ephippiorhynchus senegalensis)*. Jabiru and marabou are the largest members of the stork family. The (larger) male jabiru measures 59 in.; wing span up to 100 in.; plumage white and metallic shimmering black; bill blood-red with yellow and black cross-band; tropical Africa. Photograph from Kenya.

47. A glider is being towed by a light plane. When the desired altitude has been reached, the glider is released to continue on its own in noiseless flight.

48. Mallard drake in bridal plumage (see 29).

49. Giant kingfisher *(Megaceryle maxima)*. One of the biggest members of the kingfisher family with a wing span of easily 20 in.; plumage speckled gray-brown, underplumage red-brown and white; tropical Africa.

50. For those who love to fly, soaring in a glider plane is probably the greatest thrill of all. By taking advantage of updrafts, an experienced pilot can stay in the air for hours.

51. The turboprop engine. The propeller is almost as fast as a jet, but more economical. Shown here is the propeller of a Rolls-Royce Tyne turbine.

52. Dragonfly on a pond.

53. Hadada *(Hagedashia hagedash)*. Wing span about 55 in.; plumage dark, shimmering metallic green, red, and blue; breeds in pairs near bodies of water in tropical Africa; its name is derived from the loud warning cry it utters at the approach of man. Photograph taken at Wasa, northern Cameroon.

54. Open-bill stork *(Anastomus lamelligerus)*. Length 34 in.; wing length 17 in.; much smaller than the European white stork; plumage solid black with green and purple highlights; the two halves of the bill gape

open in the center; tropical Africa. Photographed near Wasa, northern Cameroon.

55. Tufted or squacco heron *(Ardeola ralloides)*. Length 20 in.; span 32 in.; weight 12½ oz.; reddish, yellow-brown, and white coloring; long crown feathers; breeds in southern Europe and all of Africa; winters in Africa.

56. Glider plane.

57. The *Sea Hawk,* a Royal Navy fighter plane.

58. Scooper or avocet *(Recurvirostra avosetta)* in mating posture. Length 15 in.; span 30 in.; weight 11 to 14 oz.; plumage black and white; lives near seacoast and brackish lagoons; feeds on small animals which it finds by straining mud through its upcurved bill with quick, sideways motions; breeds near the North Sea and Baltic Sea, in southern Europe, and central Asia; spends winters at the Atlantic coasts of Europe and in the Mediterranean region. Photograph from Camargue.

59. The Royal Air Force emblem and the black radar nose cone make the front of this Avro-Vulcan atomic bomber look like the face of a bird. When this giant of the skies takes off in a cloud of smoke and thunder, it is like a volcanic eruption.

60. Speckled sand grouse *(Pterocles senegallus)*. Wing span about 24 in.; plumage red-brown with black speckles; grayish-brown cap; breeds in tropical Africa. Photographed at a water hole near Garbatula, northern Kenya.

61. Like migrating birds, these Royal Air Force Hawker Hunters fly in formation at Farnborough.

62. Migrating birds in flight formation.

63. Rosy gray pelicans in flight (see 37). Photographed in Boon-Doom, Senegal.

64. Shadow bird or hammerkop *(Scopus umbretta)*. Length 22 in.; span 41 in.; plumage brown with purple sheen; bushy feather cap; lives singly near water's edge; breeds in tropical Africa; photographed at the Logone, Chad.

65. High above the waves of the air-ocean, a plane goes its lonely way. Photograph taken from a homemade Jodel-Amateur airplane.

66. Long-eared bat (see 18).

67. Dragonflies dance above the water.

68. French Fouga-Magister fighter planes at a flying jamboree in Miramas.

69. Night heron (see 1).

70. A feather, twenty times enlarged.

71. The Treble One Squadron of the Royal Air Force with Hawker-Hunter planes.

72-73. Crowned cranes (see 30).

74. Bearded or Lapland owl *(Strix nebulosa),* on its noiseless, nocturnal flight through the woods; the owl's senses are well adapted to flying in the dark and hunting at night; length 28 in.; span 56 in.; brown-gray plumage with symmetrical markings especially distinct in the circular "mask" of the face; breeds in northernmost Europe, northern Asia, and America.

75. Detail from the wing of a *Metropolitain* plane.

76. Pheasant feathers, sixteen times enlarged.

77. Black-headed heron *(Ardea melanocephala)*. Similar to the European gray heron, but somewhat smaller. Photographed in Bukavu, Congo.

78. Pheasant (see 39).

79. Scooper (see 58).

80. Brown glossy ibis or falcinel *(Plegadis falcinellus)*. Length 24 in.; span 39 in.; weight about 27 oz.; brown plumage with metallic sheen; the only European member of the ibis family; breeds in southeastern Europe; spends winters in Africa; also lives in South Asia and Australia. Photographed in Boon-Doom, Senegal.

81. *Mirage III,* French fighter planes, photographed at a flying meet in Miramas, France.

82. Buzzard's feathers, four times enlarged.

83. *Etendard IV,* French fighter plane, photographed in Miramas, France.

84. Wood ibis *(Ibis ibis)*. Plumage pink-white, wings and tail iridescent green-black; red wing stripe; naked red head; yellow bill; length about 40 in.; span 64 to 68 in.; weight 89 oz.; tropical Africa. Photographed at the Logone, Cameroon.

85. Fighter planes in a thundering dive. In modern airplanes, the sense of freedom which flying gives to man is often mingled with fear.

86. Rocket take-off.

87. Great white egret *(Casmerodius albus melanorhynchus)*. Much bigger than other snowy egrets; has no streamers at the head, but has plumage of "aigrettes" on back in breeding season; bill dark yellow; legs dark gray; length 42 in.; span 76 in.; weight about 42½ oz.; breeds in southeastern Europe, at the Neusiedler and Balaton lakes among others; also in Asia and Africa; the breed shown here is from tropical Africa. Photographed at the Logone, Chad.

88. Model of a passenger plane of the future.

89. *Mirage III,* French fighter plane, photographed at Miramas.

90. Pilots' calligraphy. In the blue sky of Farnborough, at the most important air show in the world, the "Trebel One" flight of the 92nd RAF squadron demonstrates its matchless precision.

91. Little egret (see cover).

92. Black-winged stilt (see 11-12).

Back cover: French Fouga-Magister planes.

Cover: Little egret *(Egretta garzetta)*. Length 25 in.; span 44 in.; weight 17 oz.; black bill; during breeding season has long streamer feathers on head, and plumes ("aigrettes") on back; breeds in southern Europe (Camargue, Spain), Hungary, the Balkans, Asia, Egypt; some spend winters in Africa. Photograph taken in Camargue.

1. Night heron *(Nycticorax nycticorax)*. Length 24 in.; span 43 in.; weight 26 oz.; somber coloring, gray and black-green; underside pale yellow; long narrow streamers on head; hides in shrubbery by day and begins to fish at dusk; breeds in southeastern Europe (some in central Europe), Africa, and Asia; winters in Africa. Photographed in Joyeux, Les Dombes, France.
2. Flight of Dedalus and fall of Icarus. Engraving circa 1660.
3. "Sacred ibis" of ancient Egypt *(Threskiornis aethiopicus)* survives only in Africa south of the Sahara; length 30 in.; span 46 in.; head and neck black, all other plumage white except for black wing tips and ragged, purplish iridescent shoulder feathers. Photographed at the Schari near Fort Archambault.
4. Duck feather, nine times enlarged.
5. From the first flight novel, *Journey to the Moon,* by Francis Godwin, published in 1738. In this naively imaginative tale, man is carried aloft in a contraption drawn by trained birds.
6. The desire to fly expresses itself in many ways.
7. Great ski jumpers improve the distance of their jumps by sailing with the wind.
8. Berblinger, the Tailor of Ulm, made this machine in 1811, which calls to mind the flying machines of later decades. It brought him nothing but derision from his contemporaries.
9. This 1847 flying machine, driven by guncotton, is a strange mixture of carriage, ship, and bird. Considering the heaviness of construction, it is unlikely that the machine ever got off the ground.
10. *Dreams,* an etching by Francisco Goya, from his *Proverbios.* Goya's men seem to be actually flying, but there is something spooky about them.

11-12. Black-winged stilt *(Himantopus himantopus)*. Length 15 in.; span 28 in.; weight 7½ oz.; disproportionately long red legs; plumage greenish-black and white; breeds in southern Europe, southern Asia, and Africa, where it spends the winter; prefers flat, still waters; feeds on insects, their larvae, and small molluscs. Photographed in Camargue.
13. Flamingoes *(Phoenicoperus ruber)*. Aerial photograph from Camargue.
14. A small young egret takes to the air (see cover).
15. Sketch by Leonardo da Vinci, circa 1500, showing the wing of a flying machine. This famous sixteenth-century sketch is amazing in its sophistication of form and construction.
16. "Flying dogs" are giant tropical bats with a wing span of up to sixty inches.
17. Otto Lilienthal taking off from the hangar on the Maihoehe in Steglitz, 1893. Though these early flights were brief, man was really flying by then.
18. Long-eared bat *(Plecotus auritus)*. The longer and narrower the wing, the faster and more graceful the flight.
19. This flying machine by Clément Ader in 1897 resembles a bat; its propellers are modeled on the winged seeds of plants. Man is still imitating nature.
20. Black-tailed godwits *(Limosa limosa)* on the move. Length 16 to 17 in.; span about 32 in.; weight about 10 oz.; plumage brown-gray, underplumage reddish; broad white wing streak; very long straight bill; breeds in central Europe and Asia; winters at the Mediterranean; some travel as far as tropical Africa; can be found in swamps and on the shores of lakes and ponds. Photographed near Fort Richard-Toll, Senegal.
21. The first successful flight in an enclosed machine: Henri Farman, on January 11, 1908.
22. A seagull's wings in motion.
23. Construction model of the first Rumpler-Taube ("Rumpler's Dove"), 1909. Undoubtedly, the bird served as a model for the machine; but airplane construction presents problems which cannot be solved by imitating nature.

out the photography in this book:

cques F. Ormond works with the Leica. He uses
Telyt 200-mm.; sometimes the tele-lens Hector
-mm., the Telyt 280-mm., and the Telyt 400-mm.
st of the photographs were taken on Adox films.
e feathers were photographed with a Linhof-
chnica 6×9 cm.

e Icarus legend (opposite picture 2) was taken
n Greek Legends by Gustav Schwab; the lines
Goethe (opposite picture 5) are from his letters
n Switzerland. The poem by Paul Eluard from
eorges Braque" (opposite picture 25) is from
ital des Douleurs (City of Sorrows). The lines of
delaire are from his poem "Elevation" in Les
rs du Mal (Flowers of Evil). The quotation from
l Sonnenschein (opposite pictures 88-89) was
en from his Weltstadt-Notizen, 1925 (Notes on a
tropolis, 1925).